AF706474

NEXT LEVEL INCOME

Level 1: Positive Cash Flow

By: Terrance Guillory

Table of Contents

Introduction and Summary

Thank you for choosing this eBook. I am proud of you for taking positive steps to improve your finances. In this eBook, I will guide you through the steps to achieve the first level of financial freedom. Although I cannot guarantee the exact results, if you follow these steps, you will notice significant changes in your habits and bank account. However, it's important to note that this eBook is not a get-rich-quick scheme. I aim to help you save more, reduce your debt, and increase your income. (if you are listening, keep doing those things, and you will become rich).

Now that I have told you why you should read the book let me tell you who is writing it. I'm Terrance Guillory, beast of beasts, conquer of grind, and defender of personal wealth. If none of those things get you going, then I'm Terrance Guillory I have a master's degree in business, and I am just a dude who knows a lot about finances and grind. As you can tell, I cannot turn off my sarcasm, even when writing a book professionally, so I will just highlight the sarcastic statements. (so, you can choose to read them or not, but it would be funnier if you did. You may ask yourself the difference between this book and the other personal finance books. (Well, I started the book off way better than they did, and I'm pretty sure they can't beat me in an arm-wrestling competition.) I've experienced the struggles of living paycheck-to-paycheck, but my wealth proves the system works. Join me to learn about finances, laugh, and be ready to Grind. Then Let's Kick This PIG!!!! (This is a saying I learned in the Marines, and I still think it sounds cool. Plus, it gets the people going.)

My Background

I was born in Lake Charles, LA, and grew up in a low-middle-class household. Being from Louisiana comes with a "Louisiana education." (So, if you see typos or bad grammar, you know why.) My parents worked hard but lacked financial literacy. I had to learn from books and research. (Summary: I grew up in the hood with a Louisiana education and still accrued wealth.) So, if you are willing to grind and learn, you can reach your financial targets.

During my upbringing, I learned a few valuable lessons from my environment. Firstly, it taught me that if I desired something, I had to work hard to make it happen. Secondly, I realized I had to be adaptable and think on my feet to succeed. At the age of 15, I landed my first official job at Burger King, but I was already familiar with the concept of earning money. To make ends meet, I used to do odd jobs around the neighborhood, like cutting grass. My experience at Burger King taught me the first rule of financial literacy - the importance of receiving a steady paycheck. Though my starting wage was $5.15 an hour, I knew my hard work would be rewarded with a paycheck every two weeks. This, in turn, taught me another vital lesson - the significance of saving. Since my only bill at the time was my cell phone bill, I learned a third lesson - to keep more money than I spend. These three steps are crucial if you're looking to build a solid financial foundation. (I know you will keep reading since you already paid for this book. By the way, since you brought this book, we have become best friends. YAY!!)

At the age of 18, I decided to join the US Marines because I felt that staying in Lake Charles, LA, would limit my potential, and I didn't want to attend college. The Marines taught me much about myself and shaped me into who I am today. However, it also taught me about reckless money management. Initially, I earned only

$5.15 per hour, but my paychecks increased significantly once I joined the Marines. Although I was still being paid every two weeks, I found myself spending too much money. Since the Marines provided everything except my cell phone and food, I thought my savings were insufficient. So, I decided to look closer at my financial situation and realized I wanted more from life than just women, drinks, and tattoos. (This is how we are recruited for those who have never been in the military. They also add, "See and do some cool stuff." BEST JOB EVER!!)

After delving deep into my finances, I learned lesson four: "Don't stop doing the things that make you happy. Just limit how often you do those things." Simply put, budgeting for the enjoyable things in life is essential, also known as "fun money." I wanted to spend time with my friends while limiting my expenses, so I created a "Fun Account." I deposited $240 from each paycheck into this separate account, which came with a debit card. I made a rule only to bring my Fun Account card when going out, which helped me manage my spending and still enjoy myself. (So when that particular bank account didn't have money, I didn't go out. That is called discipline, and it is precisely what you need to make financial moves.)

After serving in the Marines, I began reading several books about becoming a millionaire. However, I soon realized that these books did not provide a comprehensive guide to becoming one. In fact, one author had simply mentioned that he invested the $20,000 he earned from acting in a house. (umm, sir, most people don't have 20k just lying around.) I believe that creating a step-by-step guide to achieving financial freedom would be very useful. (basically, I'll take the good stuff from the useless books and put it effectively so you aren't wasting time. We are best friends, after all.) So far, all the books I've read emphasize the importance of having the right mindset to create wealth. A disciplined and determined mindset is indeed crucial. However, having a great action plan will significantly improve your chances of achieving your financial goals. That's why I am committed to teaching you how to create a well-crafted action plan. But it's important to remember that no matter how effective the plan is, it will ultimately be your hard work and dedication that will determine your success.

I prefer not to share my financial details because it may be intimidating for some people. I do not consider myself superior to anyone else, but I have been more successful in managing my finances. I consciously decided to learn how to accumulate wealth and have achieved that goal throughout my adult life. The formula for financial success is simple, but executing it can be challenging for some. The key is to GRIND, EARN CONSISTENT PAYCHECKS, SAVE MORE THAN YOU SPEND, AND INVEST YOUR SAVINGS WISELY. Now that you know the basic formula, if you are ready to work hard, I can teach you how to take your finances to the next level. (I'm super pumped up right now!!! I know you can't see me, but I need you to know that we are about to make some things happen. Now I need you to knock out 50 push-ups 20 jumping jacks, and give me a virtual chest bump. LFG!!!)

Now that we have finished all the fluff, I hope your boots are tied because we are about to enter the LAB. Before we start, I have a few questions. Where are my SKEPTICS?

- What if I told you you can get PAID just because you pay your bills?
- What if I told you you can get PAID to fill your gas tank?

Usually, I often get raised eyebrows because these concepts may sound ridiculous, but I will show you how to do both. So, my next question would be: Do you hate math? (If you hate math, I am so sorry you brought this book because it has a lot of numbers. The most significant number is 0, as in ZERO REFUNDS. Please don't cuss me out, and remember, we are best friends. Also, I told you I can't turn off my sarcasm.) If you dislike mathematics, don't worry; I will handle all the calculations for you. Moreover, I will provide you with charts and graphs to make it simpler for you. Remember these two formulas: either your income should be greater than your expenses, or you should save more than you spend.

I mentioned earlier that I come from Louisiana and grew up in an urban community known as "the hood." People usually call me "The Madd Scientist" because I've always worked hard in my Grind Lab. Let's talk about the concept of Grind: if you work for a company, you will receive a wage for your time. However, you won't get the full amount of your agreement. Although I received a Louisiana education, I understand basic math. If I'm paid $15 an hour and work 40 hours weekly, I should receive $600 for that pay period. ($40 * 15 = $600) It's important to note that you won't receive the full $600 due to various deductions such as taxes and insurance. So, it's a good idea to ask yourself, "How can I get my money back?" The pie chart illustrates that relying solely on a job cannot make you wealthy.

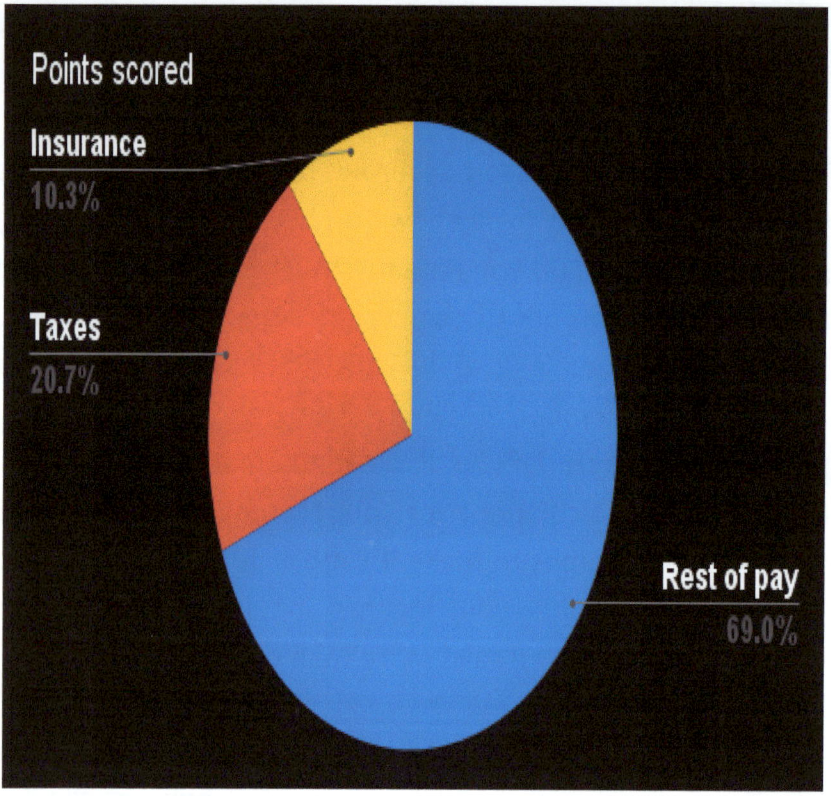

As soon as you clock in, you are starting at a disadvantage. This book aims to teach effective habits for building wealth and getting you to a positive cash flow. (How are you feeling after all that math? Does your brain hurt yet? Well, we have much more to learn.)

Fun Fact: I absolutely love checklists, and we are here to create an effective action plan. Here are a few things to strive for.

LIFE OBJECTIVES

- ○ **MAINTAIN THE QUALITY OF LIFE YOU HAVE IDENTIFIED FOR YOURSELF**
- ○ **WALK AWAY WITH RETIREMENT, AND MONEY KEEPS COMING**

This book is an excellent source of knowledge! By following its checklists, you can take the right steps toward growing your wealth. However, it's important to remember that you still need to put in hard work to achieve the results you desire. Stay committed, push through the process, and see your wealth flourish like never before!

MY OBJECTIVES

- ○ **EXPAND YOUR SAVINGS**
- ○ **LOWER YOUR BILLS**
- ○ **PAY OFF DEBT**
- ○ **INCREASE YOUR PAYCHECKS**
- ○ **CREATE A FINANCIAL TUNNEL (Generational Money Train)**

If you find the information provided so far impressive and still reading, here's a virtual high-five. I will explain every step proficiently, so take your time to review them. The steps are presented in chronological order for better understanding. Create checklists and mark them off once you achieve a goal. Remember that small positive steps often lead to significant outcomes. (If you want to make it fun, every time you mark off an achievement, do 50 pushups. Then, send yourself a self-approved email. "Boom, I just expanded my savings by $5, oh yeah!!)

Before I can help you increase your cash flow, I need to show you what prevents most people from having a positive cash flow. Don't worry; I will guide you through each financial challenge and teach you how to overcome them.

Financial Challenges

4 Main Challenges That Prevent Your Wealth

- **INFLATION**
- **FINANCIAL LITERACY**
- **TAXES**
- **BORROWING**

Challenge 1: Inflation

The economic definition of inflation refers to a general increase in prices, which results in the fall of money's purchasing power. For instance, inflation increases when the government spends more money than it has. To explain it further, if the cost of living increases, there should be a corresponding pay increase. Unfortunately, the pay rate usually does not match the inflation rate. Therefore, if expenses such as child care, groceries, and health care continue to rise, what would be the point of having a pay raise? (If you haven't caught on yet, the idea of "the American Dream" is pretty much a myth.) Unfortunately, as individuals, we cannot do much to change inflation. It would take ample small positive steps and a courageous plan of action. (Pretty much, the government needs to stop spending money that they do not have. Maybe they should read this book.)

Challenge 2: Financial Literacy

Financial literacy is the ability to make smart money decisions. Simply put, it means having the knowledge and skills to manage your finances intelligently. Unfortunately, many lack financial literacy, and some are unwilling to learn. By reading this book, you are taking a step towards improving your financial knowledge and becoming more financially literate. Virtual Hi-Five.

Challenge 3: Taxes

Living in America means that you are subject to taxation. If you have a job, you will be taxed on your income, and if you purchase something with your money, you will also be taxed. You will even be taxed if you use your already-taxed income to buy a house. Despite having already paid sales tax on the home, you will still have to pay taxes since it is on land. It is illegal to evade taxes, and I cannot help you with that as a taxed individual. However, educating yourself on financial literacy and tax laws could potentially save you some money.

Challenge 4: Debt

Many people lack financial literacy and face a money deficiency. As a result, they often resort to borrowing money to make purchases, be it through loans or credit cards. However, borrowing comes at a cost that can further bury them in debt. For instance, suppose someone wants to buy a bike for their child that costs $100. They may borrow money to purchase it if they cannot pay it in cash. However, they must pay interest on the bike's original cost since they borrowed money. ($100 in principal + $60 in interest = $160 total paid) Essentially, they just brought two bikes.

In summary, what have we learned? Firstly, we learned that inflation is something we cannot readily control. Secondly, we discovered that most people lack proficient money skills. Thirdly, we learned that we will be subject to taxation. Finally, we learned that lacking information can cost us more money. So, where do we go from here? We need to create an action plan and take small, positive steps. Your purchase of this book is already a significant first step towards increasing your financial literacy and understanding how to counteract financial challenges. (Now it's time to dive into the good stuff! You've made it this far, so you're ready for serious solutions. I know there was some fluff earlier, but trust me - it was worth it to get to this point. Let's not lie to each other, though. You know I am putting this content together in a dope manner. Oh yeah!!)

ACTION PLAN

Listen up! This is the time to buckle down and get serious. You need to focus and learn, and I need you to do 25 push-ups and 37 squats, no questions asked. I don't care if you don't understand why it's 37 squats; just do it. And remember, if you want to succeed, you need to stick to the system and complete tasks in chronological order. So, let's get to it!

MY OBJECTIVES

- ○ **EXPAND YOUR SAVINGS**
- ○ **LOWER YOUR BILLS**
- ○ **PAY OFF DEBT**
- ○ **INCREASE YOUR PAYCHECKS**
- ○ **CREATE A FINANCIAL TUNNEL (Generational Money Train)**

Earning a stable income is the initial step towards achieving financial stability. Regardless of the amount, you need a consistent flow of paychecks to take any further action toward financial growth. (Don't get mad at me. I told you from the beginning that this would be a step-by-step guide. Plus, you would be amazed at how many clients don't understand the first step.)

3 Ways We Choose To Get Paid

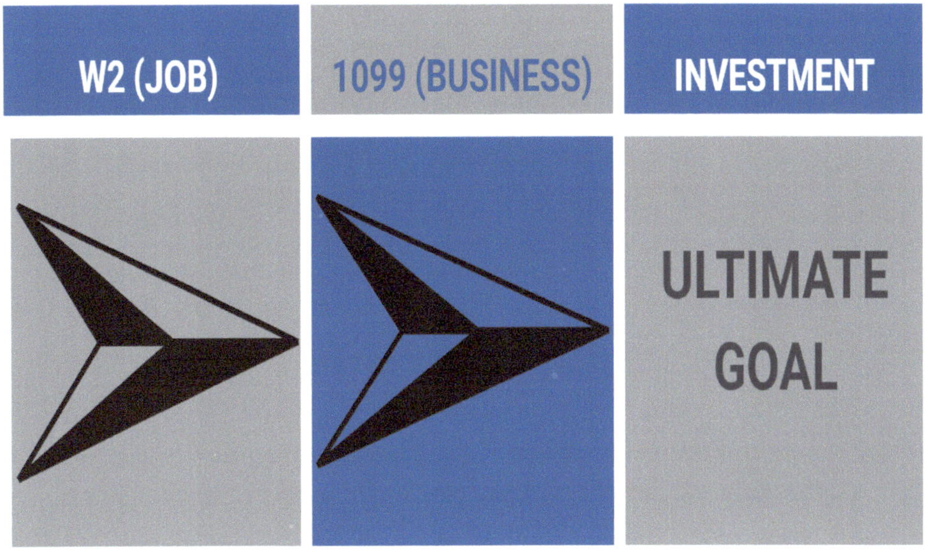

Objective 1: Expand Your Savings

What is the first thing you should pay now that you have some income?" This question can be confusing because many people think of all the bills they must pay. However, the correct answer is to pay yourself first. You are the one who works hard for your income, and you should be the first to benefit from it. This is true regardless of whether you are living paycheck to paycheck.

It's essential to develop a habit of paying yourself first. The initial amount doesn't matter, as your savings will grow over time. For instance, you can start with $10 per paycheck and put it in your savings account every time you get paid. Remember not to touch the money you save, as it's meant to be reserved for your future needs. Allow me to show you the right way to save money. If you keep withdrawing from your savings account, it defeats the purpose of having one. Trust the process, and let's work together to build your savings. (In other words, “paying yourself” means saving for yourself. It doesn’t mean spending money on yourself. 25 pushups for your mistakes.)

If you are easily attracted to shiny objects and find it hard to resist buying them, open a separate savings account where you cannot see it easily. This way, you can trick your brain into forgetting about it and saving more effectively. You may also ask your payroll office to automatically transfer a portion of your paycheck into this account. Though you will still have access to it, not looking at it can help it grow more effectively. (SET IT AND FORGET IT!!)

STOP GIVING YOUR MONEY AWAY

Once you have saved at least $10 in your savings account, it is essential to start making effective choices to prevent giving your money away unnecessarily. This requires a strong mentality, as it requires taking control of the deductions from your paychecks. Remember that every time you clock in to work, you are already at a deficit, so you must stop giving your money away and take charge of your financial situation.

Adjust Your W4

The W4 form is used by the government to take out federal taxes, of which many people are unaware. (See, this is why you brought the book; you are now better as a person. You have $10 in your bank account and understand what a W4 is.) Unfortunately, most people fill out their tax forms incorrectly, resulting in them giving the government more money than they need to. However, you can use the IRS tax withholding estimator to determine the correct withholding amount. Simply follow the link provided below, answer a few questions, and the estimator will generate the correct W4 form for you. Submit it to your payroll department, and you may see an increase in your paychecks. It's important to note that every situation is unique, so results may vary. BASIC MATH: if you have given $50 more than you need to, correcting the form will result in an increase of $50 in your paycheck.

In simpler terms, many people are overpaying the government. Correctly filling out your W4 can put more money in your pocket. If you get a paycheck raise, use the **50% Rule** to increase your savings.

https://apps.irs.gov/app/tax-withholding-estimator

The 50% rule states that whenever you get extra money, put 50% of it into savings and use the other 50% to pay off debt.

The following math will use the previous $10 a paycheck and the pay increase from the W4 form.

($10 * 2 paychecks = $20 a month in savings. Out of the $50 you received from your W4 change, $25 should go directly to savings, increasing your monthly savings to $45. The remaining 50% can be used to pay off any debt. Therefore, $45 will go into savings, and $25 will be allocated to debt.)

(see, math is pretty straightforward.)

Insurance Deductions

You may be able to increase your paycheck by adjusting your insurance coverage. Contact your provider to ensure you have the necessary coverage. Apply the 50% rule to any extra funds.

Track Your Dollars

Many people struggle to save money because they are unaware of where their money is being spent. Tracking your expenses is a great way to start understanding your spending habits. You can make necessary adjustments to your spending habits by keeping track of your finances. I suggest using a tracking system to keep track of every dollar you spend. If you prefer traditional methods, a book ledger is a great option, but if you are more tech-savvy, different apps can help you track your expenses.

Budgeting is an effective way to ensure you are spending money wisely. Begin by listing your bills, expenses, and debt in a column and input the numbers you think you are spending in the first column. Then, in the second column, put the actual amount you are paying. You can double-check the numbers by reviewing your bank statements. Once you have this information, you can make the necessary adjustments. If you're using a budgeting app, it will do it for you. Remember, you can still spend money on things you enjoy, but you may need to adjust your spending habits if the numbers don't align. For example, if you buy coffee at Starbucks daily, consider making coffee at home a few days a week to save money on coffee and travel expenses. This is also a good time to start a "Fun Account."

***Using a credit or debit card is easier to track than cash.**

Stop Helping Others

I understand that what I am about to say may be controversial, but it is important to prioritize your own financial stability before helping others. Flight attendants often remind us to put our own oxygen masks on before assisting others, and this same principle applies to financial assistance. Unless you have a comfortable surplus in your savings, it is unwise to lend money to others. Giving money alone does not solve the underlying issues that led to the financial problem. Sometimes, offering education or advice can be more beneficial than simply giving money. Over-extending yourself financially to help others can negatively affect your finances and emotional well-being. While it's important to have a balance between giving and keeping your own finances stable, it is crucial not to give more than you can afford. Remember, it's not worth going broke trying to be someone's hero.

Objective 2: Lower Your Bills

Welcome to Objective 2, where we help reduce your bills, freeing up extra money each month. Remember to implement the 50% rule whenever you have extra income. (If you still need to remember the 50% rule, you owe me 171 push-ups. COUNT THEM OUT! After you do your push-ups, then click here for the 50% rule.) Before we dive into the process of lowering your bills, it's important to understand a few key terms. These terms are bills, debt, and expenses. When I refer to "bills," I'm talking about the charges you receive for services from other companies, such as electricity, water, internet, and phone services. Regardless of your income, you will always have bills to pay. "Debt," on the other hand, refers to the money you borrowed because you didn't have enough funds available to cover certain purchases, such as car payments, mortgages, loans, and credit card balances. Fortunately, debt can be paid off and provide extra money in your pocket. I'll explain this further shortly. Lastly, "expenses" include any miscellaneous items that do not fit into the categories of bills or debt, such as gas, food, and subscription services. Now that you understand these terms, let's begin the process of lowering your bills.

Regarding bills, it's essential to understand that most companies provide the same services. For instance, Company A and Company B may offer the same type of car insurance. So, you shouldn't be loyal to any one company. In other words, if Company A offers the same car insurance for $150, why are you paying $200 to Company B? You can use this method for most bills and save money. The key is to find the cheapest price while ensuring that you still receive the value of service you need. For example, if Company A doesn't offer a rental car or towing services, you would have to weigh which one is more valuable: the extra services or the cheaper rate. With some research and changing providers, you can save a few hundred dollars each month. (I can't believe I am saying this in a financial book, "Don't be afraid to shop around." Most definitely do your research. I don't want to see any emails saying you switched companies and your bills went up.)

The following math will use the previous $10 a paycheck, the pay increase from the W4 form, and the car insurance change.

($10 * 2 paychecks = $20 a month in savings. Out of the $50 you received from your W4 change, $25 should go directly to savings, increasing your monthly savings to $45. The remaining 50% can be used to pay off any debt. Therefore, $45 will go into savings, and $25 will be allocated to debt. Company B was taking $200, while Company A will take $150, which means you now have $50. **50% rule**, half of this amount, which is $25, will be put into your savings, increasing your monthly savings to $70. The remaining $25 will go towards paying off your debt. Therefore, you will now have $70 going into your savings and $50 going towards your debt.)

Savings	Debt
$20 from paychecks	
$25 from W4 form	$25 from W4 form
$25 from car insurance	$25 from car insurance
Total: $70	**Total: $50**

Fun Fact: Did you know that you can change the billing cycle for your bills? All you have to do is call the company and request the change. For instance, if all your bills are charged to your bank account at the beginning of the month, you can ask the company to change the billing cycle. This will help you even out when your bills are paid.

***This is a good opportunity to check if the company has any promotions to help lower your bill. You don't have to remain loyal to the company, but it's worth allowing them to assist you in reducing your bill.**

TO-DO CHECKLIST:

- Have consistent income
- Open a separate savings account (if needed)
- Pay yourself first
- Adjust your W4
- Apply the 50% rule if you have a paycheck increase
- Adjust your health, dental, and vision insurance (if needed)
- Track your dollars
    - develop a budget
    - open a "Fun Account" (if required)
    - stop giving away money
    - cancel any unused subscriptions (Netflix, Xbox, Hulu, Prime)
- Lower your bills
    - find the cheapest prices **(do research)**
        - car insurance
        - phone services
        - Internet services
        - etc
- Apply the 50% rule with the extra savings

Lowering your bills is a great way to save money. You will notice a positive change in your bank account when you do this. However, it's important to maintain a disciplined mindset even after seeing the increase. You may be tempted to spend extra money on unnecessary items, but resisting this urge and remaining financially responsible is important.

Objective 3: Pay Off Debt

Now that you have achieved positive cash flow, meaning more money is coming in than going out, it is time to start paying off your debts. In my opinion, this stage is the most fulfilling because paying off debt means paying what you owe. The great thing about this stage is that once the debt is paid off, it's gone, and you have an extra paycheck. Let’s take the bicycle example we mentioned earlier. To own the bicycle, you had to pay the principal amount of $100 and the interest of $60. If you were making minimum payments of $15 a month, and the time has come to make the last payment on the account. Now, you officially own the bicycle and are $15 richer. Remember to apply the 50% rule to the $15.

There are several ways to pay off debt, but in my opinion, Dave Ramsey's Debt Snowball method is the most effective. In this guide, I will teach you how to use this method. Interestingly, I was already using this strategy before I read Dave Ramsey's book, The Total Money Makeover. I thought I had discovered something unique, but he deserves the credit since he had already published his book. However, since I am the Madd Scientist, I will add my twist to the method.

Debt Snowball With a Twist

- List all of your debt (credit cards, loans, etc.)
- Place them in order of lowest balance to highest
- Start paying off the first debt while making minimum payments on the rest
- Once the first debt is paid off, apply the 50% rule
- Use the savings to start paying debt number 2
- Repeat until all the debt is gone

Debt	Balance	Amount Due	Amount Paying
Credit card 1	$500.00	$25.00	$50.00
Credit card 2	$750.00	$50.00	$50.00
Furniture	$6,050.00	$325.00	$325.00
Car Note	$16,000.00	$250.00	$250.00
Mortgage	$188,500.00	$1,300.00	$1,300.00

***In this case, you would pay off Credit Card 1 and apply the 50% rule. Then, pay off Credit Card 2 and apply the 50% rule. Do this until all of your debt is paid off.**

***EXTRA PAYCHECKS DO NOT MEAN MORE TO SPEND. Consider opening a separate savings account for desired purchases. Make sure to save for unexpected expenses.**

Remember this: every time you pay off a debt, you give yourself an extra paycheck. If you follow the 50% rule, you'll see your bills and debt decrease while your income and savings increase. Living a debt-free life is achievable. Just keep taking small but positive steps and follow the action plan, and you'll be debt-free in no time. I can vouch for this method personally, having used it multiple times. (Buying a new car is good, but having the title of a paid-off car is like attending the jellyfish party at Spongebob's house.)

Did you know that not all debt is considered "bad debt"? If you know how to use debt responsibly, you can even make some money. Let me share with you a little trick that skeptics often overlook - the "get paid for paying your bills" strategy. Once you've paid off your credit card debt, consider paying your bills using your credit card instead of your debit card. By doing so, you can earn cashback rewards on your credit card. For instance, use your credit card instead of using your bank money to pay your phone bill. You can then pay off your credit card balance using your bank money and collect the cashback. This simple trick can help you earn some extra cash while paying your bills.

*****This is a more advanced money skill that will be explained more in book 2.*****

Objective 4: Increase Your Paychecks

(I hope you've been paying attention. I know you've been reading, at least. Have you refreshed your knowledge? Are you feeling motivated? If a chicken crossed the road, would you go across the street to slap it? I would - If I was getting an extra paycheck for it.) I have shown you how to go from living paycheck to paycheck to becoming debt-free without changing your job. Now, the exciting part begins. If you have extra paychecks, you can speed up your journey to financial freedom and build wealth faster. The only question is, what are you willing to do? From the very beginning, I have emphasized the importance of hard work. Now is the time to activate Maximum Grind and make your dreams a reality. Don't hesitate; take control of your financial future with assertiveness. Remember, you have the power to achieve anything you set your mind to. I am here to support you, but ultimately, it is up to you to do the work and make it happen.

There is so much money to be made, but you must ask yourself, "What do you have the time to do?"

- Find out what is costing you money and make it pay you.
    - your car is costing you money, so go Door Dash to pay it off
    - your house is costing you money, so get a roommate and split the bills
- Part-time job
    - shouldn't be strenuous, and it should only take up part of your time
- Youtube channel
    - there are people making money just by playing video

games.

- Side hustle
    - flip furniture
    - sell baseball cards
    - paint houses
    - cut grass
    - think of any skill you have and get paid for it

There are numerous examples available to explore, and if you are still unsure, you can search on YouTube for "side hustles." Do not hesitate to experiment with different things. If you encounter a profitable side hustle, become an expert at it and outsource it. This way, it will become a source of passive income. The fact is that if you work hard, financial gains will follow. Remember, "closed mouths don't get fed." Once you discover ways to increase your income, keep following the 50% rule until you are debt-free. Ultimately, the goal should be to create passive streams of income, which I'll explain in more detail in Book 2.

Let's calculate how much extra money can be earned by working for Doordash. For instance, if you live in Jacksonville, NC, and work for 2 hours a day, five days a week, you can earn an average of $40 per day. This equates to $20 per hour ($40 / 2 = $20), $200 per week ($40 * 5 = $200), and $800 per month ($200 * 4 = $800). Therefore, by working only 10 hours a week, you can earn an additional $800 per month. Doordash is an excellent example of a great way of Maximum Grind.

Objective 5: Create a Financial Tunnel

Congratulations on reaching this point in your journey! You should now have active savings, more paychecks, lowered bills, and less debt. As you continue to save and build your wealth, planning ahead for your future endeavors is important. Eventually, your savings will reach a point of overflow, and you'll want to be prepared for what comes next. Take the time now to strategize and make smart decisions that will set you up for success in the long run.

Let's discuss two types of money: Fast Money and Long Money. Fast Money is earned from side hustles or services. On the other hand, Long money eventually earns you more money. It's money you shouldn't touch; let it grow over time. The ultimate objective is to secure a job and convert the earnings into a business venture. The income generated from the business should be further invested in other opportunities that yield passive income. If you are not keen on running a business, you can assume the role of an investor. This approach will help you generate passive income without needing any active involvement.

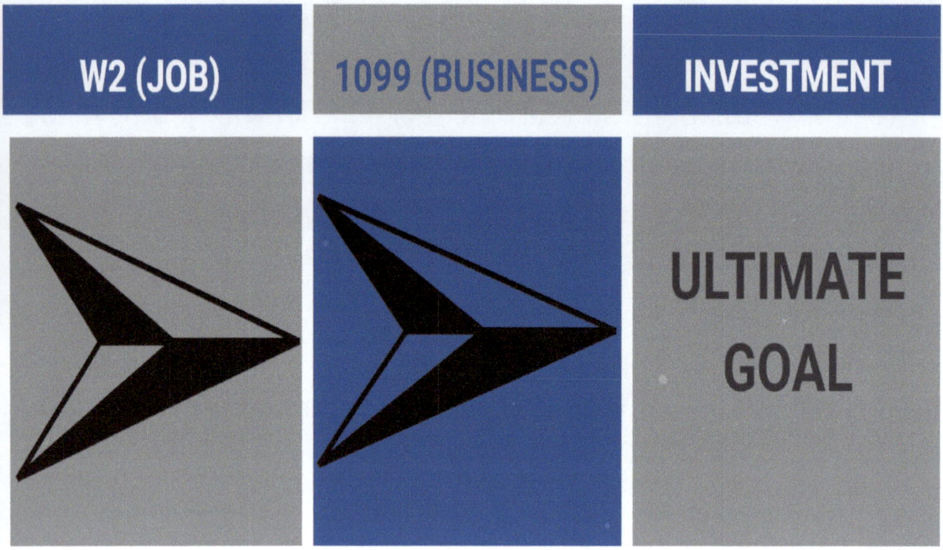

Investing your savings instead of just keeping them idle in a bank account is wise. Congratulations on your hard work! You have paid off your debts and saved some money. Now that you have a positive cash flow, planning for the future and building long-term financial stability is essential. The purpose of this book was to help you achieve a positive cash flow. If you followed the steps, you should have achieved that goal. Book 2 will provide more detailed guidance on how to build long-term wealth. (Trust me, it will take another book to explain where to put your money.) It's important to have multiple financial accounts, such as a savings account, an emergency fund, a business account, and various investment accounts. As we've discussed before, carrying debt can be expensive, so having a positive cash flow allows you to put your money to work for you and earn even more money over time.

The ultimate goal is:

- attain consistent income (get a job)
- keep more than you spend
- have active savings
- turn savings into investments
- have your investments pay you
- retire with passive income

Book 2 will guide you on utilizing interest, amassing wealth, investing wisely, and earning passive income. However, it's important to note that you should only proceed to Book 2 if you have achieved positive cash flow. Many people tend to invest without a strong financial base, but positive cash flow is the foundation for successful investments.

Conclusion

Well, Grinder, you have officially reached the end of the book. (Technically, I am still typing, so it's not exactly the end, but you get the point.) If you require a budget analysis or one-on-one coaching, please send an email to blackknightfunding@gmail.com The budget analysis will provide you with an overview of your spending habits, and together, we can devise a plan of action to help you achieve a positive cash flow. It's important to remember that building wealth is not a magic trick but a result of hard work, planning, and taking small steps toward your goals.

(I bet I will have someone who remembers I didn't tell you how to get paid for filling your gas tank. WELL, I DIDN'T FORGET.) If you want to earn cash while filling your gas tank, download the GetUpside app. Simply select a gas station from the list provided on the app, fill up your tank, and receive cash back for each purchase you make. The best part is that the app is free, so you won't be charged anything for signing up. With GetUpside, you get paid for doing something you must do anyway!

https://upside.app.link/TERRANCE3827

Ladies and Gentlemen, that is how you give a step-by-step guide to achieving positive cash flow. If you want to continue your journey and get a step-by-step guide to building wealth, please consider purchasing Book 2. If you need coaching to achieve positive cash flow, please feel free to email me. If you have completed your financial journey here, I am proud of you for taking this step and allowing me to teach you what I love. (Now you can admit I delivered that content in a dope manner. HI-FIVE!!!)

Grind and Prosper,

Terrance Guillory

MADD Scientist

NEXT LEVEL INCOME

Level 1: Positive Cash Flow

By: Terrance Guillory

www.ingramcontent.com/pod-product-compliance
Lightning Source LLC
LaVergne TN
LVHW070217220926
848482LV00030B/336